WORSHIP WITH A
TOUCH OF JAZZ

— PIANO LEVEL —
LATE INTERMEDIATE/EARLY ADVANCED

ISBN 978-1-4234-9314-3

HAL•LEONARD® CORPORATION

7777 W. BLUEMOUND RD. P.O. BOX 13819 MILWAUKEE, WI 53213

Visit Hal Leonard Online at
www.halleonard.com

Visit Phillip at
www.phillipkeveren.com

PREFACE

Worship songs, by design, are straightforward musical expressions that a congregation can learn and remember easily. The best songs in this genre, the ones that resonate over decades, have a certain "something" that speaks to the hearts of worshipers.

Jazz performers have always embraced the popular melodies of the day, using these tunes as the starting point for more sophisticated musical meanderings. In that spirit, these worship songs have been decorated in the colorful harmonies and rhythms of jazz.

Whether used in a worship service, recital, or the privacy of personal worship, I hope these arrangements will be a blessing.

Sincerely,
Phillip Keveren

BIOGRAPHY

Phillip Keveren, a multi-talented keyboard artist and composer, has composed original works in a variety of genres from piano solo to symphonic orchestra. Mr. Keveren gives frequent concerts and workshops for teachers and their students in the United States, Canada, Europe, and Asia. Mr. Keveren holds a B.M. in composition from California State University Northridge and a M.M. in composition from the University of Southern California.

CONTENTS

ALL THE EARTH WILL SING YOUR PRAISES

Words and Music by
PAUL BALOCHE
Arranged by Phillip Keveren

Flowing (♩ = 126)

mf

With pedal

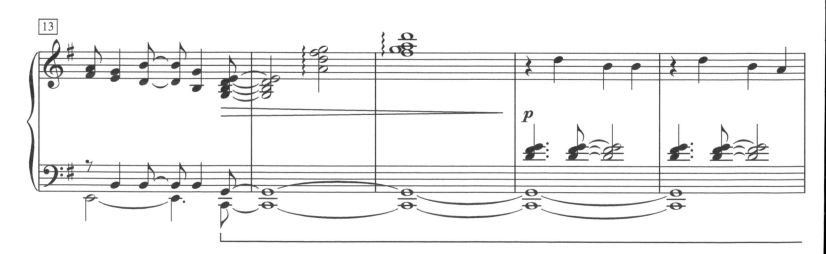

AMAZED

Words and Music by
JARED ANDERSON
Arranged by Phillip Keveren

BEAUTIFUL SAVIOR
(All My Days)

Words and Music by
STUART TOWNEND
Arranged by Phillip Keveren

Slowly, with rubato (♩. = 48)

BEFORE THE THRONE OF GOD ABOVE

Words and Music by VIKKI COOK
and CHARITIE BANCROFT
Arranged by Phillip Keveren

Reverently ($\quad$ = 72)

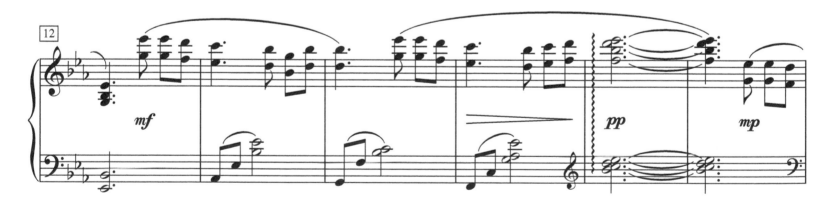

FOREVER

Words and Music by
CHRIS TOMLIN
Arranged by Phillip Keveren

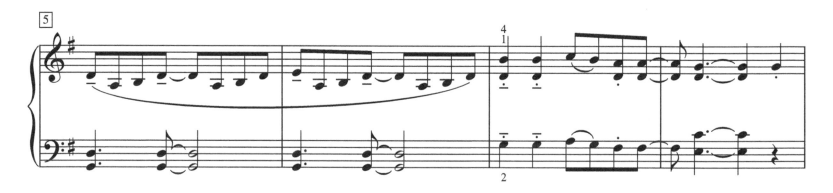

GOD OF WONDERS

Words and Music by MARC BYRD
and STEVE HINDALONG
Arranged by Phillip Keveren

HOLY IS THE LORD

Words and Music by CHRIS TOMLIN
and LOUIE GIGLIO
Arranged by Phillip Keveren

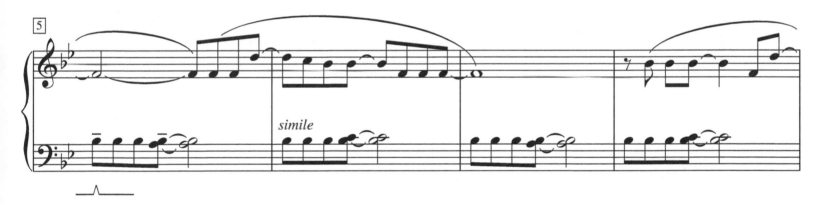

HERE I AM TO WORSHIP

Words and Music by
TIM HUGHES
Arranged by Phillip Keveren

HOLY SPIRIT RAIN DOWN

Words and Music by
RUSSELL FRAGAR
Arranged by Phillip Keveren

HOW GREAT IS OUR GOD

Words and Music by CHRIS TOMLIN,
JESSE REEVES and ED CASH
Arranged by Phillip Keveren

Peacefully (♩ = 88)

INDESCRIBABLE

Words and Music by LAURA STORY
and JESSE REEVES
Arranged by Phillip Keveren

LORD, YOU HAVE MY HEART

Words and Music by
MARTIN SMITH
Arranged by Phillip Keveren

MIGHTY TO SAVE

Words and Music by BEN FIELDING
and REUBEN MORGAN
Arranged by Phillip Keveren

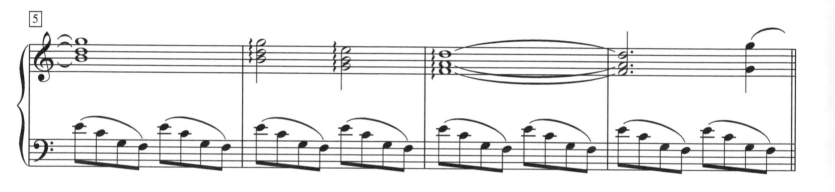

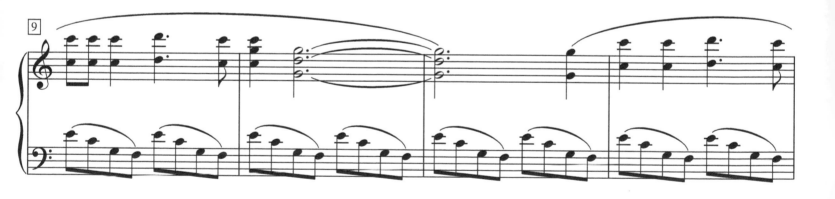

A NEW HALLELUJAH

Words and Music by PAUL BALOCHE,
MICHAEL W. SMITH and DEBBIE SMITH
Arranged by Phillip Keveren

THE POWER OF THE CROSS
(Oh to See the Dawn)

Words and Music by KEITH GETTY
and STUART TOWNEND
Arranged by Phillip Keveren

THE PHILLIP KEVEREN SERIES

PIANO SOLO

ABBA FOR CLASSICAL PIANO
00156644...$14.99

ABOVE ALL
00311024...$12.99

BACH MEETS JAZZ
00198473...$14.99

THE BEATLES
00306412...$16.99

THE BEATLES FOR CLASSICAL PIANO
00312189...$14.99

THE BEATLES – RECITAL SUITES
00275876...$19.99

BEST PIANO SOLOS
00312546...$14.99

BLESSINGS
00156601...$12.99

BLUES CLASSICS
00198656...$12.99

BROADWAY'S BEST
00310669...$14.99

A CELTIC CHRISTMAS
00310629...$12.99

THE CELTIC COLLECTION
00310549...$12.95

CELTIC SONGS WITH A CLASSICAL FLAIR
00280571...$12.99

CHRISTMAS MEDLEYS
00311414...$12.99

CHRISTMAS AT THE MOVIES
00312190...$14.99

CHRISTMAS SONGS FOR CLASSICAL PIANO
00233788...$12.99

CINEMA CLASSICS
00310607...$14.99

CLASSICAL JAZZ
00311083...$12.95

COLDPLAY FOR CLASSICAL PIANO
00137779...$15.99

DISNEY RECITAL SUITES
00249097...$16.99

DISNEY SONGS FOR CLASSICAL PIANO
00311754...$16.99

DISNEY SONGS FOR RAGTIME PIANO
00241379...$16.99

THE FILM SCORE COLLECTION
00311811...$14.99

FOLKSONGS WITH A CLASSICAL FLAIR
00269408...$12.99

GOLDEN SCORES
00233789...$14.99

GOSPEL GREATS
00144351...$12.99

GREAT STANDARDS
00311157...$12.95

THE HYMN COLLECTION
00311071...$12.99

HYMN MEDLEYS
00311349...$12.99

HYMNS IN A CELTIC STYLE
00280705...$12.99

HYMNS WITH A CLASSICAL FLAIR
00269407...$12.99

HYMNS WITH A TOUCH OF JAZZ
00311249...$12.99

JINGLE JAZZ
00310762...$14.99

BILLY JOEL FOR CLASSICAL PIANO
00175310...$15.99

ELTON JOHN FOR CLASSICAL PIANO
00126449...$15.99

LET FREEDOM RING!
00310839...$12.99

ANDREW LLOYD WEBBER
00313227...$15.99

MANCINI MAGIC
00313523...$14.99

MORE DISNEY SONGS FOR CLASSICAL PIANO
00312113...$15.99

MOTOWN HITS
00311295...$12.95

PIAZZOLLA TANGOS
00306870...$15.99

QUEEN FOR CLASSICAL PIANO
00156645...$15.99

RICHARD RODGERS CLASSICS
00310755...$15.99

SHOUT TO THE LORD!
00310699...$14.99

**SONGS FROM CHILDHOOD FOR EASY
CLASSICAL PIANO**
00233688...$12.99

THE SOUND OF MUSIC
00119403...$14.99

SYMPHONIC HYMNS FOR PIANO
00224738...$14.99

TIN PAN ALLEY
00279673...$12.99

TREASURED HYMNS FOR CLASSICAL PIANO
00312112...$14.99

THE TWELVE KEYS OF CHRISTMAS
00144926...$12.99

YULETIDE JAZZ
00311911...$17.99

EASY PIANO

AFRICAN-AMERICAN SPIRITUALS
00310610...$10.99

CATCHY SONGS FOR PIANO
00218387...$12.99

CELTIC DREAMS
00310973...$10.95

CHRISTMAS CAROLS FOR EASY CLASSICAL PIANO
00233686...$12.99

CHRISTMAS POPS
00311126...$14.99

CLASSIC POP/ROCK HITS
00311548...$12.95

A CLASSICAL CHRISTMAS
00310769...$10.95

CLASSICAL MOVIE THEMES
00310975...$12.99

CONTEMPORARY WORSHIP FAVORITES
00311805...$14.99

DISNEY SONGS FOR EASY CLASSICAL PIANO
00144352...$12.99

EARLY ROCK 'N' ROLL
00311093...$12.99

GEORGE GERSHWIN CLASSICS
00110374...$12.99

GOSPEL TREASURES
00310805...$12.99

THE VINCE GUARALDI COLLECTION
00306821...$16.99

HYMNS FOR EASY CLASSICAL PIANO
00160294...$12.99

IMMORTAL HYMNS
00310798...$12.99

JAZZ STANDARDS
00311294...$12.99

LOVE SONGS
00310744...$12.99

**THE MOST BEAUTIFUL SONGS FOR EASY
CLASSICAL PIANO**
00233740...$12.99

POP STANDARDS FOR EASY CLASSICAL PIANO
00233739...$12.99

RAGTIME CLASSICS
00311293...$10.95

**SONGS FROM CHILDHOOD FOR EASY
CLASSICAL PIANO**
00233688...$12.99

SONGS OF INSPIRATION
00103258...$12.99

TIMELESS PRAISE
00310712...$12.95

10,000 REASONS
00126450...$14.99

TV THEMES
00311086...$12.99

21 GREAT CLASSICS
00310717...$12.99

WEEKLY WORSHIP
00145342...$16.99

BIG-NOTE PIANO

CHILDREN'S FAVORITE MOVIE SONGS
00310838...$12.99

CHRISTMAS MUSIC
00311247...$10.95

CLASSICAL FAVORITES
00277368...$12.99

CONTEMPORARY HITS
00310907...$12.99

DISNEY FAVORITES
00277370...$14.99

JOY TO THE WORLD
00310888...$10.95

THE NUTCRACKER
00310908...$10.99

STAR WARS
00277371...$16.99

BEGINNING PIANO SOLOS

AWESOME GOD
00311202...$12.99

CHRISTIAN CHILDREN'S FAVORITES
00310837...$12.99

CHRISTMAS FAVORITES
00311246...$10.95

CHRISTMAS TIME IS HERE
00311334...$12.99

CHRISTMAS TRADITIONS
00311117...$10.99

EASY HYMNS
00311250...$12.99

EVERLASTING GOD
00102710...$10.99

JAZZY TUNES
00311403...$10.95

PIANO DUET

CLASSICAL THEME DUETS
00311350...$10.99

HYMN DUETS
00311544...$12.99

PRAISE & WORSHIP DUETS
00311203...$12.99

STAR WARS
00119405...$14.99

WORSHIP SONGS FOR TWO
00253545...$12.99

HAL•LEONARD®

Visit **www.halleonard.com**
for a complete series listing.

Prices, contents, and availability subject to change without notice.

The Best
PRAISE & WORSHIP
Songbooks for Piano

Above All
THE PHILLIP KEVEREN SERIES
15 beautiful praise song piano solo arrangements by Phillip Keveren. Includes: Above All • Agnus Dei • Breathe • Draw Me Close • He Is Exalted • I Stand in Awe • Step by Step • We Fall Down • You Are My King (Amazing Love) • and more.
00311024 Piano Solo.................................$12.99

Blessings
THE PHILLIP KEVEREN SERIES
Phillip Keveren delivers another stellar collection of piano solo arrangements perfect for any reverent or worship setting: Blessed Be Your Name • Blessings • Cornerstone • Holy Spirit • This Is Amazing Grace • We Believe • Your Great Name • Your Name • and more.
00156601 Piano Solo $12.99

The Best Praise & Worship Songs Ever
80 all-time favorites: Awesome God • Breathe • Days of Elijah • Here I Am to Worship • I Could Sing of Your Love Forever • Open the Eyes of My Heart • Shout to the Lord • We Bow Down • dozens more.
00311057 P/V/G $22.99

The Big Book of Praise & Worship
Over 50 worship favorites are presented in this popular "Big Book" series collection. Includes: Always • Cornerstone • Forever Reign • I Will Follow • Jesus Paid It All • Lord, I Need You • Mighty to Save • Our God • Stronger • 10,000 Reasons (Bless the Lord) • This Is Amazing Grace • and more.
00140795 P/V/G $22.99

Contemporary Worship Duets
arr. Bill Wolaver
Contains 8 powerful songs carefully arranged by Bill Wolaver as duets for intermediate-level players: Agnus Dei • Be unto Your Name • He Is Exalted • Here I Am to Worship • I Will Rise • The Potter's Hand • Revelation Song • Your Name.
00290593 Piano Duets $10.99

51 Must-Have Modern Worship Hits
A great collection of 51 of today's most popular worship songs, including: Amazed • Better Is One Day • Everyday • Forever • God of Wonders • He Reigns • How Great Is Our God • Offering • Sing to the King • You Are Good • and more.
00311428 P/V/G $22.99

Hillsong Worship Favorites
12 powerful worship songs arranged for piano solo: At the Cross • Came to My Rescue • Desert Song • Forever Reign • Holy Spirit Rain Down • None but Jesus • The Potter's Hand • The Stand • Stronger • and more.
00312522 Piano Solo..................................$12.99

The Best of Passion
Over 40 worship favorites featuring the talents of David Crowder, Matt Redman, Chris Tomlin, and others. Songs include: Always • Awakening • Blessed Be Your Name • Jesus Paid It All • My Heart Is Yours • Our God • 10,000 Reasons (Bless the Lord) • and more.
00101888 P/V/G $19.99

Praise & Worship Duets
THE PHILLIP KEVEREN SERIES
8 worshipful duets by Phillip Keveren: As the Deer • Awesome God • Give Thanks • Great Is the Lord • Lord, I Lift Your Name on High • Shout to the Lord • There Is a Redeemer • We Fall Down.
00311203 Piano Duet $12.99

Shout to the Lord!
THE PHILLIP KEVEREN SERIES
14 favorite praise songs, including: As the Deer • El Shaddai • Give Thanks • Great Is the Lord • How Beautiful • More Precious Than Silver • Oh Lord, You're Beautiful • A Shield About Me • Shine, Jesus, Shine • Shout to the Lord • Thy Word • and more.
00310699 Piano Solo $14.99

The Chris Tomlin Collection – 2nd Edition
15 songs from one of the leading artists and composers in Contemporary Christian music, including the favorites: Amazing Grace (My Chains Are Gone) • Holy Is the Lord • How Can I Keep from Singing • How Great Is Our God • Jesus Messiah • Our God • We Fall Down • and more.
00306951 P/V/G $17.99

Top Christian Downloads
21 of Christian music's top hits are presented in this collection of intermediate level piano solo arrangements. Includes: Forever Reign • How Great Is Our God • Mighty to Save • Praise You in This Storm • 10,000 Reasons (Bless the Lord) • Your Grace Is Enough • and more.
00125051 Piano Solo.................................$14.99

Top Worship Downloads
20 of today's chart-topping Christian hits, including: Cornerstone • Forever Reign • Great I Am • Here for You • Lord, I Need You • My God • Never Once • One Thing Remains (Your Love Never Fails) • Your Great Name • and more.
00120870 P/V/G...$16.99

The World's Greatest Praise Songs
Shawnee Press
This is a unique and useful collection of 50 of the very best praise titles of the last three decades. Includes: Above All • Forever • Here I Am to Worship • I Could Sing of Your Love Forever • Open the Eyes of My Heart • and so many more.
35022891 P/V/G $19.99

HAL•LEONARD®
www.halleonard.com

P/V/G = Piano/Vocal/Guitar Arrangements